UPDOG

EXTREME SKATEBOARDING CHALLENGES

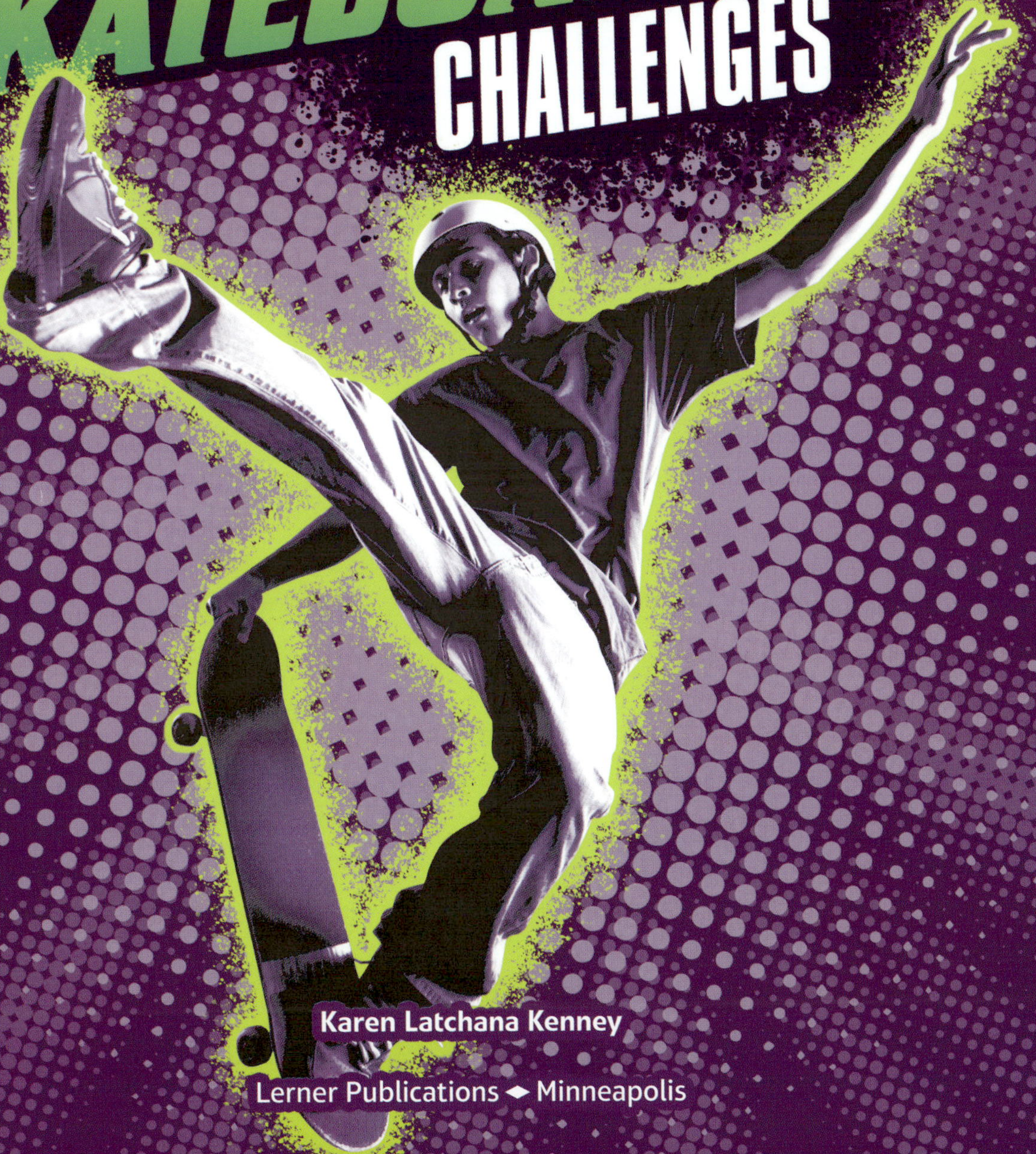

Karen Latchana Kenney

Lerner Publications ◆ Minneapolis

Lerner Publications Company
An imprint of Lerner Publishing Group, Inc.
241 First Avenue North
Minneapolis, MN 55401 USA

For reading levels and more information, look up this title at www.lernerbooks.com.

Main body text set in ITC Franklin Gothic Std.
Typeface provided by Adobe Systems.

Editor: Rebecca Higgins **Designer:** Viet Chu

Library of Congress Cataloging-in-Publication Data

Names: Kenney, Karen Latchana, author.
Title: Extreme skateboarding challenges / Karen Latchana Kenney.
Description: Minneapolis : Lerner Publications, 2021. | Series: Extreme sports guides (UpDog Books ™) | Includes bibliographical references and index. | Audience: Ages 8–11 | Audience: Grades K–1 | Summary: "Extreme skateboarding challenges demand balance, strength, and speed. Readers will be thrilled by skaters and their daring stunts"—Provided by publisher.
Identifiers: LCCN 2020005015 (print) | LCCN 2020005016 (ebook) | ISBN 9781541590465 (library binding) | ISBN 9781728418148 (ebook)
Subjects: LCSH: Skateboarding—Juvenile literature. | Extreme sports—Juvenile literature.
Classification: LCC GV859.8 .K46 2021 (print) | LCC GV859.8 (ebook) | DDC 796.22—dc23

LC record available at https://lccn.loc.gov/2020005015
LC ebook record available at https://lccn.loc.gov/2020005016

Manufactured in the United States of America
1-47565-48095-7/2/2020

Table of Contents

Big Air Gold

The MegaRamp isn't for every skateboarder. Only the best ride its steep walls in the X Games.

Bob Burnquist has claimed big air gold ten times.

BOB BURNQUIST

big air: a high jump in skateboarding, BMX biking, or snowboarding

Big air is one extreme skateboarding event. Riders use huge ramps to vert.

vert: a skateboarding style using ramps with steep sides for tricks

Downhill and freestyle are other extreme events. Riders do wild tricks and skate fast to compete.

downhill: an event where skateboarders speed down a slope

freestyle: a skateboarding routine done on flat ground

UP NEXT!

How to train hard.

Extreme Training

Before athletes can do tricks, they learn how to skateboard. They have to be fearless.

Athletes train at skate parks. They ride into half-pipes and skate on rails.

half-pipe: a U-shaped ramp used in skateboarding

skate park: a park with structures and surfaces for skateboarding

They get better at tricks. They try 360s, ollies, and 720s.

ollie: a trick where skateboarders kick the board's tail down while jumping

Extreme skateboarders rush down hills. They fly off big ramps.

Skateboarders train at gyms too.

Bio Break!

Name: Lacey Baker

Age: 28

Hometown: Covina, California

Claim to fame:

- Won seven medals in Skateboard Street events at X Games
- On the first USA Skateboarding team for the Olympics

They lift weights and work their cores.

core: the muscles in a person's torso

Skateboarding Hacks

- You will fall. Get up. Great skateboarders practice (and fall) tons. Make sure to wear a helmet when you skate!
- At first, skip the skate park. Train in open lots with smooth pavement.
- Get a good skateboard. The right equipment helps.
- Break in your skateboard. Cruise around on your first ride. Save the tricks for later.

UP NEXT!

The hardest competitions for tough athletes.

Skateboarding Competitions

The X Games is one of the biggest extreme sports competitions. It happens once a year.

Skateboarders compete in a stadium. It's set up with ramps and a course.

In street competitions, athletes race through obstacles.

Skaters ride half-pipes. They do difficult tricks to win.

World Cup Skateboarding holds big competitions all around the world.

Extreme skateboarders take risks. Their skills win them medals at the toughest competitions.

Glossary

big air: a high jump in skateboarding, BMX biking, or snowboarding

core: the muscles in a person's torso

downhill: an event where skateboarders speed down a slope

freestyle: a skateboarding routine done on flat ground

half-pipe: a U-shaped ramp used in skateboarding

ollie: a trick where skateboarders kick the board's tail down while jumping

skate park: a park with structures and surfaces for skateboarding

vert: a skateboarding style using ramps with steep sides for tricks

Check It Out!

Abdo, Kenny. *Skateboarding*. Minneapolis: Abdo Zoom, 2018.

Ducksters: Skateboarding
https://www.ducksters.com/sports/extremeskateboarding.php

Exploratorium: Skateboard Science
https://www.exploratorium.edu/skateboarding/

Funbrain: Extreme Air
https://www.funbrain.com/games/extreme-air

Kenney, Karen Latchana. *Extreme Snowboarding Challenges.* Minneapolis: Lerner Publications, 2021.

Wolny, Philip. *Extreme Skateboarding.* New York: Rosen, 2020.

Index

Photo Acknowledgments

Image credits: rogistok/Shutterstock.com (background); A.RICARDO/Shutterstock.com, p. 4; Rick Kern/WireImage/Getty Images, p. 5; Cameron Spencer/Getty Images, p. 6; Dorosh/Shutterstock.com, p. 7; Peyton Fulford/Moment/Getty Images, p. 8; lzf/Shutterstock.com, pp. 9, 11, 21; THEGIFT777/iStock/Getty Images, p. 10; wavebreakmedia/Shutterstock.com, p. 12; Brian Gove/Getty Images, p. 13; GaudiLab/Shutterstock.com, p. 14; Yoann MORIN/Shutterstock.com, p. 16; A. Einsiedler/Shutterstock.com, pp. 17, 20; How/Getty Images, p. 18.

Cover: Blend Images - Erik Isakson/Getty Images; rogistok/Shutterstock.com.